Mel Bay's

GUIDE TO THE CAPO TRANSPOSING, & THE NASHVILLE NUMBERING SYSTEM

by Dix Bruce

1 2 3 4 5 6 7 8 9 0

Visit us on the Web at www.melbay.com — E-mail us at email@melbay.com

Table of Contents

Dix Bruce is a musician and writer from the San Francisco Bay Area. He has authored over thirty books, recordings, and videos for Mel Bay Publications. He does studio work on guitar, mandolin, and banjo and has recorded two LPs with mandolin legend Frank Wakefield, eight big band CDs with the Royal Society Jazz Orchestra, his own collection of American folk songs entitled *My Folk Heart* on which he plays guitar, mandolin, autoharp and sings, and a CD of string swing & jazz entitled *Tuxedo Blues*. He contributed two original compositions to the soundtrack of Harrod Blank's acclaimed documentary *Wild Wheels*. He has released two CDs of traditional American songs and originals with guitarist Jim Nunally.

Dix Bruce arranged, composed, played mandolin, and recorded music for the CD ROM computer game "The Sims" for the Maxis Corporation. "Sims" is the newest entry in the best selling "Sim City" series. His music is featured on a virtual radio station within the game.

Photo by Gene Tortora

Guide to the Capo, Transposing, and the Nashville Numbering System

by Dix Bruce

Welcome to the book with the ungainly title "Guide to the Capo, Transposing, and the Nashville Numbering System." Yes, it's a mouthful, but you'll soon find that all three subjects are closely related and that learning about one will help you understand each of the others.

In practical terms, once you've worked through this book, you'll know how a capo works and why, you'll understand the basic rudiments of music theory which will help you transpose chords and melodies with or without a capo, and you'll be conversant enough in the elements of the Nashville Numbering System to discern a song's chord progression and to communicate it with your fellow players using chord numbers.

So, let's get started. Meet you at the coda!

The Chromatic Scale

Before we can tackle using the capo, how to transpose, or the Nashville Numbering System, we'll need to discuss some of the basic concepts of how our system of music works. Just about everything in music starts with two scales: **the chromatic scale** and the **major scale**.

The **chromatic scale** is made up of twelve notes C, C♯/D♭, D, D♯/E♭, E, F, F♯/G♭, G, G♯/A♭, A, A♯/B♭, B, C and includes all of the notes we use to describe or write down music. Each note is one half step from its neighbor up or down. On a standard piano keyboard a half step is the

distance from one key to its immediate neighbor, black or white. On a standard fretted instrument (excluding instruments like the mountain dulcimer) one half step is the distance from one fret to the next.

A chromatic scale can be played on a piano keyboard by starting on any key and moving up or down the keyboard one key at a time (including both black and white keys) until all twelve notes are played. You can play a chromatic scale on a fretted instrument by starting on any fret and moving up or down the fingerboard one fret at a time. Of course,

4

depending upon where you start, you may run out of keys or frets! Look at the diagrams of a piano keyboard and guitar fingerboard below. There are other notes in between the frets on a guitar or the keys on a piano,

like those you get when you bend a guitar string in blues or rock, but for our purposes here we'll call the chromatic scale complete.

In the listing of the chromatic scale above and on the keyboard and

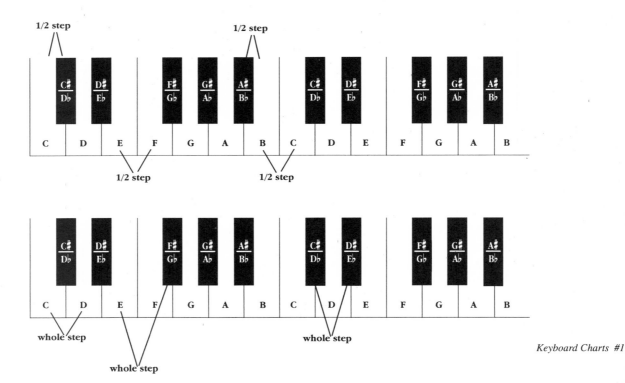

Keyboard Charts #1

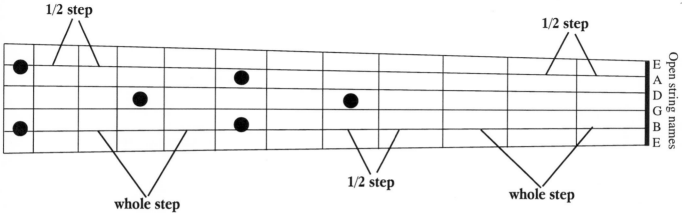

Fingerboard Chart #1

fretboard diagrams you'll notice that some notes are given two names, for example, C♯/D♭. Either can be used to name the note. C♯ and D♭ are **enharmonic** names for the same note. Depending upon the root key and context, the note may be referred to as one or the other.

It's important that you know the names of the notes on your guitar. You can figure them out easily if you start with the names of the open strings. In standard guitar tuning they are, string one through six, highest to lowest pitch: **E, B, G, D, A, E**. (How about "Easter Bunnies Greet Duckies After Easter." Yeah, I know. Think of a better one and I'll send you a free bumper sticker. See my address on page 56.) Once you know the open string notes, you can simply overlay the chromatic scale on the fretboard and count up by half steps / frets to identify the fretted notes,

wherever they fall on the fretboard. Both the open and fretted notes are identified in the guitar fingerboard on page 6.

You'll notice on both the keyboard and fingerboard that there are no enharmonic notes between the E and F or the B and C. I don't know that there's any logical explanation for this, it's just the way it is! There's a half step interval between E and F and between B and C. On the piano keyboard these are the only sets of white keys without a black key in between. So, there are no such notes as B♯, C♭, E♯, or F♭. However, as I mentioned above, you may find a context where someone refers to B♯ (which is C), C♭ (B), E♯ (F), or F♭ (E).

You might also notice that the chromatic scale listed above has thirteen notes, not twelve as I mentioned. This is because the first note is

6

repeated as the last. Both are C notes, but the second is the distance or **interval** of an **octave** above the first.

The repetition of these groups of chromatic notes continues both up and down the keyboard or fretboard, in terms of pitch, to the limits of the instrument. Of course sounds in nature ascend and descend infinitely but we only recognize those within the limits of our hearing. If you're a dog or a whale, you can presumably hear higher and/or lower notes than humans. If you're a dog or whale and currently reading this book, please contact me. We have lots to talk about. For example, where did you get the money to buy this book? That reminds me of a joke. Kangaroo goes into a bar. Bartender sees him and asks what the kangaroo's pleasure is. The kangaroo answers, "I'll have a beer." Bartender is amazed but figures he can make a little dough on a naive drinking kangaroo so he brings the beer and says to the kangaroo "That'll be $17.00." Kangaroo reaches into his pouch and pulls out a twenty dollar bill. Bartender brings him the change and says, "You know, we don't get many kangaroos in here." Kangaroo chugs the beer, sweeps the change into his pouch and answers, "At these prices, I'm not surprised!" But enough levity.

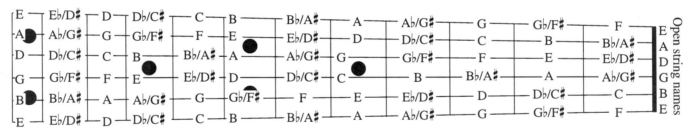

Fingerboard Chart #2

The E chromatic scale shown on the next page in standard musical notation and guitar tablature ascends from lower pitches to higher. Chromatic scales may also be described as descending. Same scale, different direction. Try playing this E chromatic scale. Understanding how it works on the guitar is the key to understanding how to use the capo.

E chromatic scale

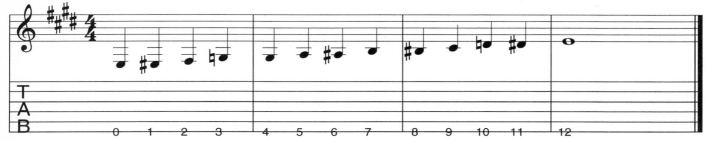

The scale shown above is called an E chromatic scale since it begins on an E note. The first note, in this case an E, is the root note and names the scale. All of the E chromatic scale notes are playable on the sixth or lowest pitched guitar string from the open (unfretted) E to the twelfth fret E an octave higher. But we don't **have** to play all the notes on the sixth string and it's actually much easier to switch strings. One of the great qualities of the guitar is that we can play most notes at more than one position on the fretboard and save unnecessary hand movement. Here's what the same E chromatic scale looks like when it's played on strings six, five, and four. As you play it, you'll notice how much easier it is to reach the notes than the previous scale with all the notes on one string.

E chromatic scale #2

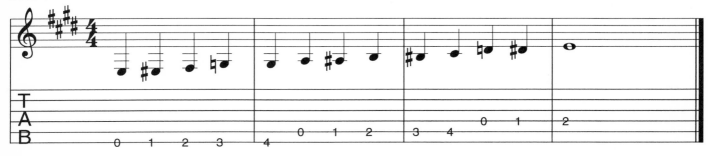

An A chromatic scale would have the same notes as the E chromatic, but it would begin and end on the A note and proceed in this order: A, A♯/B♭, B, C, C♯/D♭, D, D♯/E♭, E, F, F♯/G♭, G, G♯/A♭, A. We can begin a chromatic scale on any of the twelve notes of the chromatic scale. Here are the A and the C chromatic scales in standard notation and tablature. They can either ascend or descend. Play through them. Once you memorize them, they'll make great warm-up exercises.

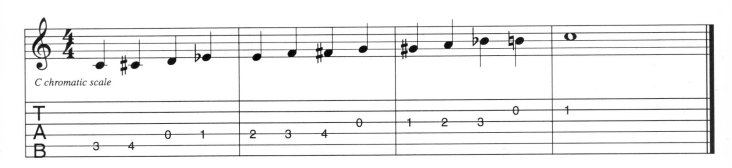

C chromatic scale

A chromatic scale

The Major Scale

We derive the **major scale** from the chromatic scale. In the chromatic scale, each note is one half step from its neighboring notes. We can refer to this one half step distance as an **interval** of one half step. So, the interval between any two consecutive notes in a chromatic scale is one half step, which is also the interval from one fret to its neighbor.

We all know the major scale as the familiar "do-re-me-fa-so-la-ti-do." What's important about the major scale and what differentiates it from other scales is the particular arrangement of intervals between its eight notes. Major scales use both half step and whole step intervals between notes in a predictable and defined pattern: one whole step between notes 1 & 2, 2 & 3, 4 & 5, 5 & 6, 6 & 7 and one half step between notes 3 & 4 and 7 & 8.

We can begin a major scale on any note of the chromatic scale, on piano, guitar, or any other instrument. If we apply the intervals above, we'll define a major scale from the first or **root** note and that root note will name the scale.

Let's try it starting on a C note. Here's the C major scale with the whole step/half step pattern and scale numbers diagrammed. Notice that scale numbers one and eight (both "do," a.k.a. "The Homer Simpson Note") are the same note an interval of one octave apart.

	C	D	E	F	G	A	B	C
	do	re	me	fa	so	la	ti	do
Scale #	1	2	3	4	5	6	7	8
		wh	wh	1/2	wh	wh	wh	1/2

The C major scale is especially easy to see on the piano keyboard. It uses only the white keys.

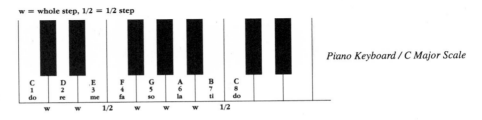

Piano Keyboard / C Major Scale

Play through the C major scale shown below in musical notation and TAB. It's not as easy to visualize on the guitar, but being guitarists, we live for the challenge! Keep in mind that this isn't the only C major scale that can be played on the guitar. This is just one of many. There are others at several different positions. As you develop as a player you discover them and all make great warm-up exercises.

Let's move on to the G major scale and start by diagramming it :

	G	A	B	C	D	E	F#	G
	do	re	me	fa	so	la	ti	do
Scale #	1	2	3	4	5	6	7	8
		wh	wh	1/2	wh	wh	wh	1/2

Here's the G scale on the guitar.

Here's what the G scale looks like on the piano.

w = whole step, 1/2 = 1/2 step

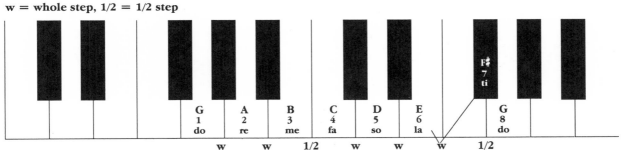

Unlike the C major scale which used only the white keys on the piano, we have to change the F to an F♯ (a black key) in order to preserve the half step interval between notes seven and eight. If we didn't sharp the F natural note, the interval between F and G, notes 7 and 8 of the G scale, would be a whole step rather than a half step, and we wouldn't have a G major scale. So, there's only one note different in the G and C major scales: F in the C major scale and F♯ in the G major scale. And, as you'll see, the key signature of the key of G will have one sharp in it.

By the way, all of these piano keyboard diagrams are designed to help with your social life. Sure, you can play the guitar, everybody knows that. Now that you know at least two major scales on the piano, use this knowledge to your advantage at your next party. At a lull in the proceedings, casually stroll over to the Steinway and with a thoughtful look on your face, play the C major scale. Before you play anything, be sure to loosen up your hands by shaking them wildly for a few seconds. Next run both hands through your hair and pause for about eight seconds, staring intently at the keyboard. The trick is to play it as seriously as possible evoking either a haughty classical or hipster jazz attitude. You'll be amazed at the number of people that will say, "Chuck (or Charlene), I knew you could play the guitar, but you're wonderful on the piano." You heard it here first folks.

We can begin a major scale on any of the twelve tones of the chromatic scale and build it by applying the "whole, whole, half, whole, whole, whole, half" interval pattern between the eight notes. The chart below shows the notes that comprise all the major scales. Just like chromatic scales, major scales can ascend or descend.

Major Scale Chart

		Major scale	1	2	3	4	5	6	7	8 (1)
Key	-		do	re	me	fa	so	la	ti	do
C	none	C	C	D	E	F	G	A	B	C
F	1 - ♭	F	F	G	A	B♭	C	D	E	F
B♭	2 - ♭	B♭	B♭	C	D	E♭	F	G	A	B♭
E♭	3 - ♭	E♭	E♭	F	G	A♭	B♭	C	D	E♭
A♭	4 - ♭	A♭	A♭	B♭	C	D♭	E♭	F	G	A♭
D♭	5 - ♭	D♭	D♭	E♭	F	G♭	A♭	B♭	C	D♭
G♭	6 - ♭	G♭	G♭	A♭	B♭	C♭	D♭	E♭	F	G♭
C♭	7 - ♭	C♭	C♭	D♭	E♭	F♭	G♭	A♭	B♭	C♭
C♯	7 - ♯	C♯	C♯	D♯	E♯	F♯	G♯	A♯	B♯	C♯
F♯	6 - ♯	F♯	F♯	G♯	A♯	B	C♯	D♯	E♯	F♯
B	5 - ♯	B	B	C♯	D♯	E	F♯	G♯	A♯	B
E	4 - ♯	E	E	F♯	G♯	A	B	C♯	D♯	E
A	3 - ♯	A	A	B	C♯	D	E	F♯	G♯	A
D	2 - ♯	D	D	E	F♯	G	A	B	C♯	D
G	1 - ♯	G	G	A	B	C	D	E	F♯	G

The far left hand column identifies the key the related major scale defines and names. It's easy: the D major scale defines the key of D major, etc. The second column in from the left tells how many sharps (#) or flats (♭) are needed to make the "whole, whole, half, whole, whole, whole, half" interval pattern between the eight notes. For the key of D we need two sharps. The D row is the second up from the bottom. If we follow the row over to the right, we can see that those

two sharped notes are F# and C#. This same number of sharps or flats will be present in the **key signature** of the piece when it's written. For example, if you see three sharps in the key signature, the song is in the key of A. See the examples below. (The key signature appears just to the right of the clef sign and to the left of the **time signature** on a music staff. Time signatures are not always included in the staff.) We'll discuss more about keys and key signatures later.

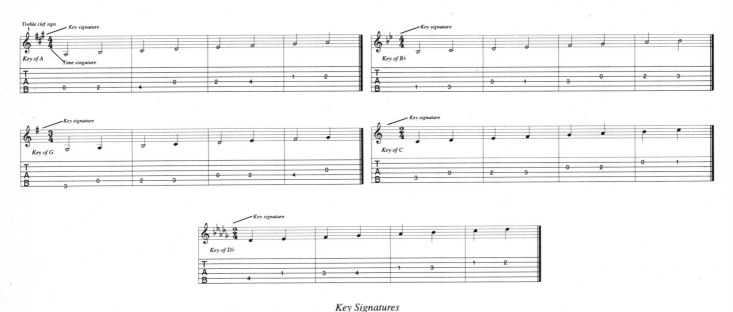

Key Signatures

Going back to the scale chart, the third column in from the left gives the name of the major scale which is also the root, "do," or first note of the scale. Reading horizontally, you can find all of the notes of all the major scales. Remember that notes can be named enharmonically and that the B♭ scale could also be thought of as the A♯ scale.

These different scales give us the twelve different keys* in music. You can sing "do-re-me-fa-so-la-ti-do" starting on any of the chromatic notes. Some scales will be within your vocal range, others will not. Likewise, you can begin a song's melody on any note and find the perfect place where it fits your vocal range. Since melodies are different, you won't necessarily find one key that's "your key," rather you'll try to find the key that's best for you on a particular melody.

So how does all this relate to using a capo? You're kind of impatient, aren't you? No problem, I understand. We're guitar players, after all, and as such, the world is our oyster! So, I fully realize that you'd much rather be out in that world playing music, driving fancy cars, counting your money, etc., than reading my deathless prose. Anyway, hang on, capos are next on the agenda and they'll make much more sense now that you've had this brief music theory lesson.

(*) You'll notice that there are fifteen keys/scales, not twelve. Some are listed with their enharmonic twins: D♭ = C♯; G♭ = F♯; C♭ = B. So, we only have twelve different scales.

CDs, videos, and instructional books by Dix Bruce: (For songlists and full details, contact Musix, PO Box 231007, Pleasant Hill, CA 94523. E-mail: MUSIX1@aol.com)

You Can Teach Yourself Country Guitar by Dix Bruce book & CD, tape, or video set

BackUp Trax: Basic Blues for Guitar by Dix Bruce, book & CD set (Mel Bay) Jam all night long with the newest TRAX set of hot blues grooves: Delta, Country, Urban, Modern, it's all here! You play all the leads and the band never gets tired!

Doc Watson & Clarence Ashley 1960-62 for Guitar (book & CD sets of transcriptions: chords, melodies, lyrics, Doc's solos & rhythm playing, incredible repertoire).

Beginning Country Guitar Handbook-Basic Flatpicking by Dix Bruce book & CD set

String Band Classics: The Fuzzy Mountain String Band for Mandolin, Guitar *(book & CD sets of transcriptions: chords, melodies, lyrics, solos).*

BackUp Trax: Swing & Jazz Vol. I book & CD set. Jam all night long with a great band. You play all the leads and the band never gets tired!

BackUp Trax: Old Time Fiddle Tunes Vol. I book & CD set. Jam all night long with the band on old time and fiddle tunes.

BackUp Trax: Traditional Jazz & Dixieland book & CD set. Jam all night long with the band on the basic Dixieland repertoire.

BackUp Trax: Early Jazz & Hot Tunes book & CD set. Jam all night long with the band on more traditional jazz standards.

You Can Teach Yourself Mandolin book & CD, tape, or video set.

Great Mandolin Pickin' Tunes book and cd set from the QwikGuide series.

Basic Country Flatpicking Guitar video *(Stefan Grossman's Guitar Workshop).*

Basic Swing Guitar video *(Stefan Grossman's Guitar Workshop).*

From Fathers to Sons CD by Dix Bruce & Jim Nunally of folk, bluegrass, & hot guitar picking *(Musix CD/C 104).*

The Way Things Are CD by Dix Bruce & Jim Nunally. More hot picking & great new songs by the duo. *(Musix CD/C 105).*

My Folk Heart CD by Dix Bruce, solo & small group, traditional American folk music *(Musix CD/C101)*. With Jim Nunally, Tom Rozum, and John Reischman.

Tuxedo Blues CD by Dix Bruce, string swing & jazz *(Musix CD/C102)*. With Bob Alekno on mandolin, David Balakrishnan on violin, Mike Wollenberg on bass.

The Capo

A capo is a clamp that can be positioned on the guitar neck to effectively "shorten" the length of the strings. We place the capo in any fret, slightly behind the metal fret wire, adjust it until there's a minimum of buzzes and rattles, and play. The resulting chord or melody will sound higher than the same thing played without the capo. For example, if an E chord is played with the capo clamped on the third fret, the resulting **sound** will be a G chord, even though the player is holding what looks like an E chord.

The great advantage of this is that you can learn a melody, chord progression, or song in one key and with a capo raise it by half steps (remember, one fret equals one half step) to almost any other key without relearning it. In this way you can accommodate your own voice or other singers and players who perform a tune in a different key than you know. Let's explore how this works.

The vibrating length of standard guitar strings between the nut (see the diagrams below) and saddle is about twenty five and one half inches.

Guitar Diagram #1

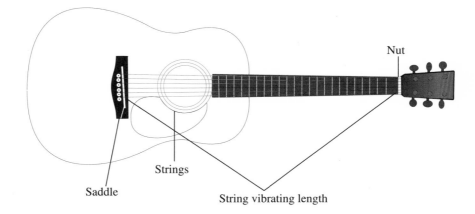

Nut

Strings

Saddle

String vibrating length

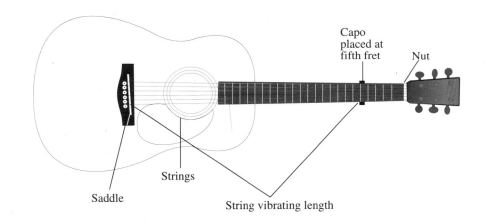

Capo placed at fifth fret

Nut

Saddle

Strings

String vibrating length

Guitar Diagram #2

When you place a capo between any two fret wires on the fingerboard, it temporarily takes the place of the nut and shortens the vibrating length of the strings by the distance you capo up from the nut. (By the way, to place the capo in the third fret, it should be adjusted to be right behind the third metal fret wire.) The shorter the string, the higher pitched sound it makes. That's what you'd expect. After all, a tiny piccolo makes higher pitched sounds than a huge tuba. So anything played capoed will sound higher than the same thing played without the capo. But how much higher?

Each fret spans an interval of one half step and each fret is one half step from its immediate neighbor, just like the notes of the chromatic scale. Let's look again at the E chord played with the capo at the third fret. In this case the capo is three frets above the guitar nut so the resulting chord is three half steps above the standard E chord. By consulting the chromatic scale shown below, we can count up three half steps from E and land on G. From the scale below, you can see that one half step above E is F, whether we're talking about notes or chords. F$\sharp$/G$\flat$ is two half steps above E. (Remember that F$\sharp$ and G$\flat$ are two different names for the same note.) Since one fret equals one half step, we can see that putting the capo on the third fret will give us the sound of a G chord when we play an E chord. If the capo were on the fourth fret, the resulting chord would be G$\sharp$ or A$\flat$ and so on up the neck.

Frets / 1/2 steps	E	F	F♯/G♭	G	G♯/A♭	A	A♯/B♭	B	C	C♯/D♭	D	D♯/E♭	E
	0	1	2	3	4	5	6	7	8	9	10	11	12

Here are a couple more examples. Put the capo on the second fret and play a G chord. What is the **sound** of this chord? Look at the chromatic scale representation above and count up two half steps from G. We go up two half steps because our capo, is in the second fret. The actual sound of a G chord capoed at the second fret is an A chord.

Now put the capo at the fifth fret and play an E chord. What is the sound of this chord? Again, count up five half steps from E. We go up five half steps because our capo is in the fifth fret. The actual sound of an E chord capoed at the fifth fret is an A chord.

Finally, put the capo at the seventh fret and play an Am chord. What is the sound of this chord? Count up seven half steps from A. We go up seven half steps because our capo, is in the seventh fret. The actual sound of an Am chord capoed at the seventh fret is a Em chord. (Since our original chord is minor, the capoed chord will also be minor.)

This kind of practice will get you used to the idea of using a capo and figuring out what sound a capoed chord or melody makes. The more you calculate the resulting effects of capoing at different frets, the easier it will become to do on the fly without much figuring. To help you get started, here's a chart that shows capoed chord positions. It's a little something I like to call "The Capo Chart" on page 18. Simply match up the chords you want to hear with the chord you want to play and place the capo accordingly.

The first column on the far left ("Chord Held") shows the name of the chord you'll make. The columns to the right tell you what the sound of the held chord will be with the capo at different frets. For example, find the F chord in the "Chord Held" column. Now stay in that horizontal row and move over two columns to the right, under the "2" heading and you'll find a G. This means that if you put the capo on the second fret and play the F chord, it'll sound like a G chord. Here's another example. A D chord capoed at the fifth fret will give the sound of a G chord. Again, find the D chord in the "Chord Held" column. Follow that horizontal row to the right five columns and you'll see a G chord. Chords are listed with their enharmonic names, for example, an A♯ chord can also be referred to as a B♭ chord.

Any chord with the letter names shown in the chart, regardless of suffix, can be used (For example, C7, Cm, C9, C dim, Cm7, C aug, C major 7, etc.). The chart only shows fret numbers to 12 and at that point the whole thing starts all over again. Unless you have an electric guitar with huge gaping cutaways, it's unlikely that you'll capo anywhere near the twelfth fret. You still have to fit your hand in front of the capo! Most guitars won't allow capoing much above the ninth fret. Guitars will show their unwillingness to be held this tightly and this high up by playing very out of tune.

Capo Chart

Actual Sound of Chord

Chord held

Capo on Fret #	1	2	3	4	5	6	7	8	9	10	11	12
C	C♯/D♭	D	D♯/E♭	E	F	F♯/G♭	G	G♯/A♭	A	A♯/B♭	B	C
C♯/D♭	D	D♯/E♭	E	F	F♯/G♭	G	G♯/A♭	A	A♯/B♭	B	C	C♯/D♭
D	D♯/E♭	E	F	F♯/G♭	G	G♯/A♭	A	A♯/B♭	B	C	C♯/D♭	D
D♯/E♭	E	F	F♯/G♭	G	G♯/A♭	A	A♯/B♭	B	C	C♯/D♭	D	D♯/E♭
E	F	F♯/G♭	G	G♯/A♭	A	A♯/B♭	B	C	C♯/D♭	D	D♯/E♭	E
F	F♯/G♭	G	G♯/A♭	A	A♯/B♭	B	C	C♯/D♭	D	D♯/E♭	E	F
F♯/G♭	G	G♯/A♭	A	A♯/B♭	B	C	C♯/D♭	D	D♯/E♭	E	F	F♯/G♭
G	G♯/A♭	A	A♯/B♭	B	C	C♯/D♭	D	D♯/E♭	E	F	F♯/G♭	G
G♯/A♭	A	A♯/B♭	B	C	C♯/D♭	D	D♯/E♭	E	F	F♯/G♭	G	G♯/A♭
A	A♯/B♭	B	C	C♯/D♭	D	D♯/E♭	E	F	F♯/G♭	G	G♯/A♭	A
A♯/B♭	B	C	C♯/D♭	D	D♯/E♭	E	F	F♯/G♭	G	G♯/A♭	A	A♯/B♭
B	C	C♯/D♭	D	D♯/E♭	E	F	F♯/G♭	G	G♯/A♭	A	A♯/B♭	B

Capo Chart

There are quite a variety of capos available these days from simple elastic bands to more elaborate Dr. Seuss inspired spring clamps. They all work in the same general way though each has its strengths and weaknesses. Depending upon how you use them, and on which of your guitars, you may find that certain capos have more of a tendency to buzz at certain frets. Others may squeeze the strings out of tune. Still others may be too large and get in the way of your fretting hand. The best approach is to try one capo until you find its limits and then try another!

I've used most of the capos on the market but my favorite for about twenty years has been the Shubb Capo. Rick Shubb set out to make a better mousetrap...er...capo, and actually succeeded. His capos work better and last longer than any I have tried. They tend to be a bit more expensive than some of the other models available, but you'll lose your Shubb capo before it wears out. And, Rick keeps innovating and improving them. His latest, the **S1**, shown in the next column, has a wheel and soft plastic pads that make moving and adjusting the capo quieter and smoother than ever before. Check it out!

As you can surmise from the music theory we've worked through, I believe that it's very important to know how and why a capo works and to be able to identify capoed chords and keys. Of course you can use a capo to your heart's content without any of this fancy book learnin'. All you have to do move the capo around the fingerboard until you find the sound you like. This comes in handy if you learn a song from a book or maybe a jam session and find that your voice is too low or too high for the chords you know. No problem! Capo to the rescue! All you do is try the capo at a few different positions until you find a set of chords that will accommo-

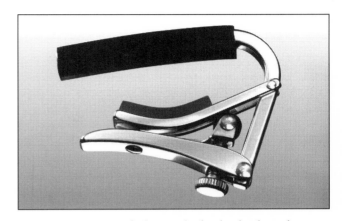

date your voice. Once you find it, simply play the chords you know.

Another great use for the capo will be in fitting a chord progression you know in one key to someone else's voice and another key. Again, all you have to do is try the capo at a few different positions until you find the one that fits best for the voice you're backing up.

I apply a basic rule of thumb to help me find the best capo position for any voice. I have a pretty typical male vocal range. If I'm backing up a similar voice, I start out assuming that they'll sing a song in about the same key that I sing it in. If I'm backing up a typical female voice, I'll start out with the capo at the fifth or seventh fret. I may have to adjust it one way or the other, but I'm usually in the ball park. If you're a female backing up a male, start with the same assumptions and try the capo at fret five or seven first. This realization will also come in handy when we learn to transpose keys without the capo later in this book. For example, if I sing *The Crawdad Song* in the key of G, a typical female voice will probably be pitched an interval of a fourth or fifth above me in pitch and sing in the key of C or D. We'll get back to this later on.

The capo can be an artistic tool as well as a practical one. Play an open B♭ chord. Now capo at the third fret and play a G chord. The sound of that capoed chord will be a B♭ chord. Notice how different they sound? You may prefer one over the other for a particular effect on a song. (If you're a beginner, you may find it much easier to play the capoed G than the regular B♭ chord.) Or, you may find that a particular picking pattern works with a G chord but is impossible with a B♭ chord.

When two guitarists work together one can play open (non-capoed) chords while the other plays capoed up. My guitar duo partner and I, Jim Nunally, do this quite frequently. The result is a very full sound. For example, one of us will play an open C while the other plays a G capoed at the fifth fret. (You can check out our CDs on Musix, PO Box 231005, Pleasant Hill, CA 94523 • email: musix1@aol.com) Both chords sound like C with slightly different, though complementary, **voicings**. This is often done on country recordings. One guitarist plays without a capo using open chords while the other capos as high as possible to get a high, zingy rhythm guitar sound. Or you can both play capoed at different frets using completely different sets of chords. You just have to decide what key you want to perform the song in.

Let's work through this concept. You'll need to get together with a guitarist friend to explore the following. Play an open G chord. Now capo at the third fret and play an E chord which now sounds like a G. Notice the special qualities of each? Now we'll apply this technique to *Will the Circle Be Unbroken* (pages 22 & 23). To start out we'll play it in the key of E. The song has only three chords: E, A and B7. Practice the song until you can play it without the music.

Once you're familiar with *Will the Circle Be Unbroken*, work through the following exercises with a picking buddy. One of you should play the song as written, the other should place the capo at the fourth fret. Now the questions is, what chords should the capoed guitarist play? Just for the fun of it, try playing a capoed E against the uncapoed E. It'll probably sound a little...shall be say... "modern" and chances are you won't like the sound much. Why? Look at the capo chart above and figure out what the **sound** of the E chord capoed at the fourth is. To do that, first find the E chord in the far left hand column. Then follow over four spaces to the fourth fret column where you'll see G♯/A♭. A G♯/A♭ chord played with an E chord just doesn't sound very good. Let's find out what does.

Since our first uncapoed chord is E, we need to find a chord in the fourth fret column that will give us the same sound as the uncapoed E. To do that, go back to the chart and find the fourth fret column. The first row / box has an E in it and if we follow this row over to the left to the first column we find a C. That means that if we play a C chord capoed at the fourth fret, it will make the **sound** of an E chord. Try it with the uncapoed E. It should sound pretty good.

Now you know which capoed chord to play with the uncapoed E chord. Using a pencil, write a "C" next to or above every E chord in the *Will the Circle Be Unbroken* music.

Next we need to find a fourth fret capoed chord that fits with the uncapoed A chord. Again, find the fourth fret column on the chart and follow down until you find the A. Then follow that row over to the left to see what chord you need to hold capoed at the fourth fret to sound like an A chord. It's the F chord. Write in an F chord everywhere you see an A chord in the music.

Finally we need to find a fourth fret capoed chord that fits with the uncapoed B7 chord in the original *Will the Circle Be Unbroken*. Once again, go to the fourth fret column of the chart and follow down until you come to a B. Then follow that row over to the left and you'll find that you need to play a G chord capoed at the fourth fret. But that's not quite correct yet. Since we started with a B7, the new chord also needs to be a 7, in this case a G7. Whatever the suffix of the original chord, 7, minor, 6, etc., you need to match it in the substitute chord. Write a G7 everywhere you see a B7 in the music. As you play through *Will the Circle Be Unbroken* with your partner, one should read the set of original chords, one the penciled chords.

Let's work through another capo position while were cooking. This time place the capo at the seventh fret. Again the first chord we need to find a substitute for is the uncapoed E. Find the seventh fret column of the chart and follow down until you find the E. Follow this row to the farthest left hand column and you'll find an A chord. Just like you did before, pencil an "A" in everywhere you have an E chord in the original music. Don't erase the chords you've already written, just carefully add these. (And remember, in music as in everything else, neatness counts!) Once you've done this, find the substitute chords for the original uncapoed A and B7 and write them in. You should find that D is the seventh fret substitute for the A chord and E7 is the substitute for the B7. Now try this set of chords along with the uncapoed set.

At this point, both you and your picking buddy have three choices of capo positions and chords. One of you can play the original uncapoed chords while the other plays the first set of different chords with the capo at the fourth fret. Or, one of you can play the original uncapoed chords while the other plays the second set of different chords with the capo at the seventh fret. Finally, one of you can play the fourth fret chords while the other plays the seventh fret chords. Be sure to try this last one. As you experiment with the different combinations, listen to the unique voice or timbre each combination gives. Obviously you can go through this same procedure for any capo position and you'll find a vast range of different possible sounds.

While capos are a wonderfully practical and artistic tool, they do have their drawbacks. One is that when moved they usually require you to re-adjust the tuning of your guitar. I've used just about every type of capo on the market; elastic straps, spring clamps, thumb screw clamps, etc., and they all send your tuning out of whack. That can be a pain in the neck, especially for your audience, if you're on stage and switching positions a lot — you'll spend more time tuning than playing. (That's where the jokes come in!) It seems to be more of a problem the higher up the neck you go. I also find that certain combinations of guitars and brands of capos have more or less of a problem in this line. As you develop as a guitarist, you'll explore the capabilities of both your capo and guitar and the learn how to minimize the tuning problems through trial and error.

It's also tough sometimes to get rid of all the fretboard buzzes and rattles as you move a capo to different positions. There will be times when you just can't get it tight enough to get a good clean sound on

Will the Circle Be Unbroken

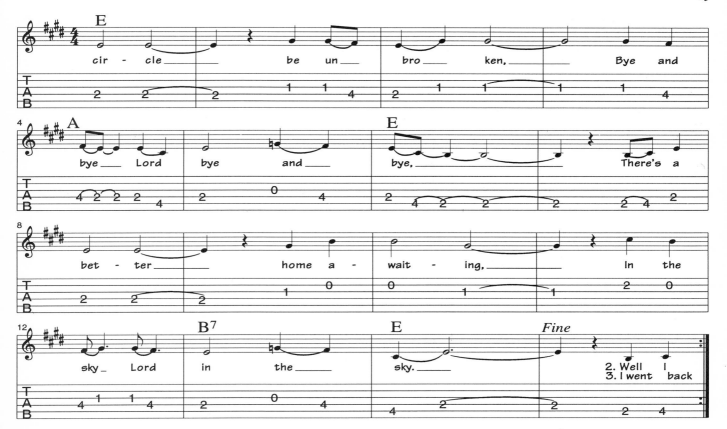

every string. When that happens, the natural tendency is to tighten your capo. You can torque that baby down to about 300 P.S.I. (Of course if you do, you'll have serious tuning problems and a broken guitar neck.) It's usually not so much a question of tightness as it is of moving the capo around to find just the right angle on the fingerboard. I try to place the capo as close as I can to the higher fretwire. For example, if I capo at the third fret, I place the capo as close to the third fretwire as I can. Then I jiggle it around while picking strings until the buzzes are gone.

Probably the most serious drawback to using the capo is that it can become a crutch and a roadblock to learning transposition theory. We'll get into transposing without a capo in the next section of this book but in the meantime, be sure to try to play tunes in other open keys before you "capo up." You'll find your general guitar knowledge will develop far faster than if you always immediately resort to slapping on the capo.

As you add songs to your repertoire, try using the capo at different positions and in different keys. If you get confused, consult the capo chart. With practice you'll eventually be able to create arrangements in which you mix open and capoed chords without looking at the chart.

At this point, congratulations are in order! You're already transposing with the help of a capo! Be sure that you understand why it works because the next section of this book will build on and expand that knowledge. In fact, the goal of the following section is to teach you how to transpose without using a capo since there will be situations when the use of a capo is impractical or impossible. Read on! But first, remember that all work and no play makes Jack a dull boy. (I got this joke from my pal, the great guitarist Duck Baker, in case you don't think it's funny. Note to Duck: a nimble mind is a terrible thing to waste!) Storekeeper sees a penguin standing at the door sobbing. Storekeeper says, "What's the matter little fellow?" Penguin says, "I can't find my father." Storekeeper glances up and down the street and asks, "What does he look like?"

Quiz so Far

1. Suppose you want to play a song in the key of B♭ but only know the chords in the key of E: E, A, and B7. Where will you put the capo?

2. What are the names of the open string notes, from string one to string six, highest pitched to lowest?

3. Name these notes: a) string 1 fret four; b) string 2 fret 1; c) string 3 fret two; d) string 4 fret twelve; e) string 5 fret three; f) string 6 fret six.

4. Our singer wants a song to be played in the key of F but wants neither you nor I to play it uncapoed. Name two capo / key combinations we can play.

5. How many 1/2 steps are between a) a G and the next A above it? How many 1/2 steps between b) an F and the next E below it?

6. Are the author's jokes brilliant or what?

7. What note is a whole step below D♯?

8. How many roads must a man walk down before they call him a man? *(All answers on page 44.)*

More Transposing

We just explored the use of the capo as a way to change keys and accommodate the different pitch ranges of voices. We slap the capo on a given fret, say fret three, and it raises the pitch or sound of the chord we strum by that number of (in this case three) half steps. Capos offer an easy way to transpose music but they're ultimately quite limiting: they knock your guitar out of tune, they take time to move, and if you're not careful they can become an obstacle to learning about music theory and getting along without one. Not only that, there are many transposing situations where they won't be of much help.

For example, let's say you're at a Loretta Lynn concert in Branson, MO. (Here you'll have to use a little imagination for several reasons, most importantly my attempt at light, often hilarious banter. It may be that you are not a country music or Loretta Lynn fan. As remote as that possibility might seem to me, feel free to substitute Barbra Streisand, Celine Deon, Frank Sinatra, Billy Joel, Michael Stipe, Aretha Franklin, Deborah Harry, one of those guys from the Beastie Boys or Blink 182, or whoever floats your boat for the purposes of this fantasy and book. Back to Loretta.) Her rhythm guitar player has missed the band bus. The band can't play without him (a fantasy within a fantasy) and there's no one in the auditorium who can save the show. The first song on Loretta's set list is *Will the Circle Be Unbroken* (Stay with me on this...) "Wait a minute," you think, "I know *Will the Circle Be Unbroken* in the key of E. I can save the show!" You push your way through the crowd and grab a guitar. The bass player says, "Key of D, kick it off!" "No problem, Slick,"

you say, "I got my capo in my pocket." Only then do you realize that you are doomed. You break out in a cold sweat as you realize there is no way in heaven or hell that you can capo that guitar at the tenth fret. What will you do, WHAT WILL YOU DO? You learn a little music theory, that's what. Read on, fast.

The trick is to look at chords generically and see how they function within a key. As it turns out, the system is very regular and makes perfect sense. Eventually we'll relate it to what's often called "The Nashville Numbering System" so called because of its use in studios in Nashville to communicate chord progressions among musicians where standard music notation is often not written down or read. However, the term "Nashville Numbering System" is a somewhat limiting name since the system is used universally by musicians of all styles from blues to classical. Makes no difference what you call it, "The Numbering System" is in use everywhere musicians play and it's very important that you understand what it means and how it is used even if you don't plan to spend any time in Nashville. After we explore a little of the background of the Numbering System, we'll look at it in depth in the Nashville context.

When we talked about capos, we used the chromatic scale or half step scale: C, C♯/D♭, D, D♯/E♭, E, F, F♯/G♭, G, G♯/A♭, A, A♯/B♭, B, C, twelve different notes in all. (You'll recall that notes listed with a slash, like C♯/D♭, are different names, *enharmonic spellings*, for the same note.) You won't find notes called E♯/F♭ or B♯/C♭ no matter how long you look. By definition the space between E and F, B and C is one half step. Some know-it-all music Einstein will delight in pointing out that C♭ is really a B natural note and that E♯ is really just an F. (Technically true but almost never important.) To review, notes on adjacent frets follow this chromatic pattern. For example, notes on the first string E begin with the open E. The first fretted note is F, second fretted note is F♯/G♭, third fretted note is G, and so on up to the twelfth fret E, which is an octave higher than the open string E. Above the twelfth fret, the pattern repeats beginning with the F note at fret thirteen. This is why the capo works the way it does.

As you learned earlier, we derive our major scale from the chromatic scale. We can begin this scale on any pitch, any note on the fretboard or keyboard, and apply a specific set of intervals or distances between each of the notes in the whole and half step pattern shown below. "Wh" stands for whole step and "1/2" means half step. These intervals define a major scale and a key. The C major scale has the following notes:

	C		D		E		F		G		A		B		C
	do		re		me		fa		so		la		ti		do
Scale #	1		2		3		4		5		6		7		8
		wh		wh		1/2			wh		wh		wh		1/2	

Here's the C major scale in music and TAB:

Notice that the 1 and 8 are the same note one octave apart. One half step equals one fret on the guitar, one whole step equals two frets. In a major scale there are whole steps between notes 1 and 2, 2 and 3, 4 and 5, 5 and 6, 6 and 7. There are half steps between notes 3 and 4 and 7 and 8. We number notes in the scale using Arabic numerals and refer to notes in a scale as the "one," "four," "seven," etc. Here's the G major scale:

	G		A		B		C		D		E		F♯		G
	do		re		me		fa		so		la		ti		do
	1		2		3		4		5		6		7		8
		wh		wh		1/2			wh		wh		wh		1/2	

The G major scale in standard notation and tablature:

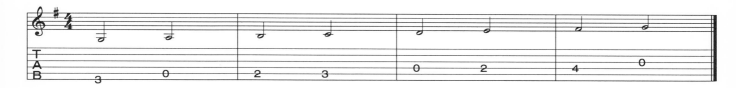

We can relate this to the fretboard and play an E major scale on the first string by ascending the fingerboard with the whole step — half step pattern. Start with the open first string E, go up a whole step or two frets to the second fret F#, two more frets up to fret for G#, etc. to the twelfth fret octave E. Here's what the E major scale looks like with fret numbers listed below:

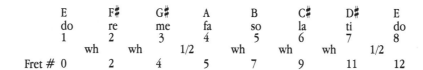

We build chords and keys on the notes of the major scale. The chords shown below are constructed using only the notes from the major scale, in this case the G major scale. We're not limited to only these chords, in fact we can change the minors shown to dominant seventh chords, but these are the chords that use **only the notes of the major scale**. For now, don't worry if you don't see your favorite chords listed below.

	G	Am	Bm	C
Chord #	I	ii	iii	IV

D	Em	F#°	G
V	vi	vii	VIII/I

Chords in keys are labeled with Roman numerals: uppercase for major chords (I, IV, V), lower case for minor and diminished chords (ii, iii, vi, etc., the seventh is diminished and indicated by °). The VIII and I chords are the same and they name the key. (We refer to notes in a scale as well as chords in a key by numbers. The only difference is context.) The Numbering System is all about referring to chords in keys by their numbers rather than by there letter names. This system recognizes that every chord has a certain function within a key: a "I" ("one") a "vi" ("six") a "V" ("five") and so on. So if I tell you that the chord progression to a song is I, IV, V, I, ("one, four, five, one") in the key of G you'll know that I mean to play the chords G, C, D, G. Suppose we need to play the same song in the key of C. The Roman numerals will apply and you'll know to play the chords C, F, G, C since in the key of C, the C chord is the I, the F is the IV, the G is the V, etc. I should mention that in the Nashville Numbering System chord charts are usually written using Arabic numerals (1, 2, 3, etc.) and not Roman numerals (I, ii, iii) like you'll find in the more traditional approaches to the study of music theory. When we learn about the Nashville System we'll do as they do in Nashville (when in Nashville, y'all) but right now for clarity we'll use Arabic numbers when we refer to notes in scales and Roman numerals when we're discussing chords in a key. Let's explore this concept more and get back to Loretta — the audience is getting ugly!

You know the chords to *Will the Circle Be Unbroken* in the key of E. They are E, A, and B7. Loretta needs to sing the song in the key of D. What chords will you play? Before we can transpose, we need to know what Roman numerals to assign to the chords in the key of E. Look at the chart below and you'll see that the E, A, and B7 chords are the I, IV, and V respectively. What are the I, IV, and V chords in the key of D?

(Key of E) E	F#m	G#m	A
I	ii	iii	IV
(Key of D) D	Em	F#m	G

B	C#m	D#°	E
V	vi	vii	VIII/I
A	Bm	C#°	D

To play the song in the key of D, play a D chord instead of the E (both are I chords); play a G chord instead of the A chord (both are IV chords); and play an A7 chord instead of a B7 chord (both are V chords). The chord suffixes must match so if the V chord is a V7 in the original key, it needs to be a V7 in the transposed key. Write in the new transposed chords in *Will the Circle Be Unbroken* and play it in the transposed key of D. Now get up on that stage and save the show for Loretta! Yeah, I know it's a bit of a fantasy, she probably starts her shows with *Coal Miner's Daughter.* But we can dream, can't we?

All About Keys

Before we move on to another song, let's talk a bit more about keys. In order to understand transposing and the Nashville Number System, we'll need to know what key a song is in. Scales define keys. The C major scale defines the key of C and a melody using the notes of the C major scale can be said to be "in the key of C." Using the notes of the C major scale in a melody anchor that melody in a certain pitch range and tonality. We could sing or play the same melody one whole step higher and find ourselves in the key of D. Different keys will ac-

commodate different ranges of vocal and instrumental pitches. And, as you already know, the same song played with the same chords capoed and uncapoed will be in two different keys.

The $64,000 question then is, how can we tell what key a song is in? The one surefire way is to analyze the key signature. As you'll remember from page 13 the key signature of a song is the area between the clef sign, in this case the treble clef, and the time signature, here 4/4, 2/3, or 3/4.

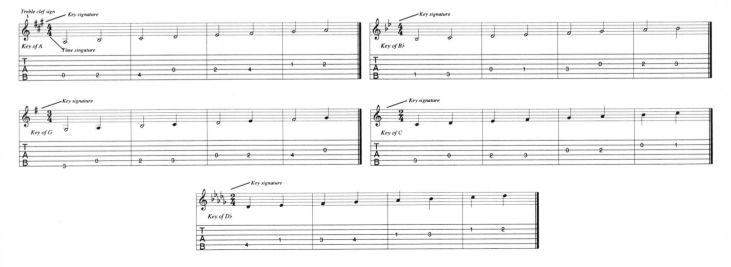

The key signature can have sharps, flats, or neither, and these flats or sharps affect notes played throughout the song. If there's a flat sign in the key signature on the B line of the staff (third up from the bottom), all the Bs in the song will be played as B♭, unless you're directed to do otherwise. The number of sharps or flats uniquely defines the key, for example, if a song has one flat in the key signature, the song is in the key of F. If the key signature has no sharps or flats, the song is in the key of C. If it has only one sharp, the song is in the key of G. Take another look at the key signature examples on the previous page and compare them to the major scale chart on page 12.

Eventually you'll want to memorize all the key signatures but for now you can look them up on the major scale chart (page 12) or scale and chord chart (page 39). In both charts the far left column identifies the key. The next column to the right shows the key signa-ture (number of sharps or flats) of that key. The scale chart will also tell you the major scale of each key, which is directly related to the key signature. The transposition chart goes further and identifies the chords built on each key's major scale.

How are key signatures derived? You'll recall that when we first talked about major scales we said that a major scale could start on any note of the guitar or piano. The remaining seven notes are determined by applying specific intervals between the notes: whole steps between notes 1 & 2, 2 & 3, 4 & 5, 5 & 6, 6 & 7 and half steps between 3 & 4 and 7 & 8. That unique pattern is often referred to as "whole, whole, half, whole, whole, whole, half" and gives us the familiar major scale "do-re-me-fa-so-la-ti-do" with those defined intervals between notes. The key of C major has no sharps or flats in its key signature. That's because the C major scale has no sharped or flatted notes.

C	D	E	F	G	A	B	C
do	re	me	fa	so	la	ti	do
1	2	3	4	5	6	7	8
	wh	wh	1/2	wh	wh	wh	1/2

Here's a musical excerpt in the key of C showing the key signature for the key of C. Not much to it, right? Again, you'll see no sharps or flats in the key signature of the key of C because the C major scale has no sharped or flatted notes in it.

Look at the G major scale. In order to maintain the proper intervals ("whole, whole, half, whole, whole, whole, half") of a major scale we need to raise the F natural to an F♯ so the interval between notes 7 & 8 will be a half step.

	G	A	B	C	D	E	F♯	G
	do	re	me	fa	so	la	ti	do
Scale #	1	2	3	4	5	6	7	8
		wh	wh	1/2	wh	wh	wh	1/2

The F♯ is the only changed note (compared to the C major scale) so when we write the key signature for the key of G major, it will have only one sharp and that one sharp will be placed so the top line of the staff, the F line, will pass through the middle of the little tic-tac-toe symbol.

Here's a musical excerpt in the key of G showing the key signature.

Let's look at another key signature. How about B♭? Here's the B♭ scale:

	B♭	C	D	E♭	F	G	A	B♭
	do	re	me	fa	so	la	ti	do
Scale #	1	2	3	4	5	6	7	8
		wh	wh	1/2	wh	wh	wh	1/2

In order to have the proper "whole, whole, half, whole, whole, whole, half" pattern of intervals we see that two notes have to be flatted: the B and the E. Just as with the other keys, we'd expect the key signature for the key of B♭ to have two flats on the appropriate lines or spaces, in this case the B line (third up from the bottom) and the E space (fourth up from the bottom).

So, key signatures are defined by the corresponding major scale and once we know a key signature we can identify the major scale, chords, and key of any song. Meanwhile, horse walks into a juice bar. Waiter says, "Why the long face?"

More About Key Signatures

There are couple of rules that help me remember and identify key signatures. First of all, memorize the fact that the absence of sharps or flats in a key signature means the song is in the key of C. Also, one flat in a key signature means the song is in the key of F. Once you know those two facts, the other keys can be determined as follows. For sharp keys (that is, keys with sharps in the key signature) find the farthest sharp sign to the right, determine which line or space it's on and count up one half step. For example, the key signature below has two sharps. (Of course you could instantly look it up on the scale or transposition charts, but play along, humor me and you'll learn something pretty cool.) The farthest sharp to the right is on the third space up from the bottom of the staff, the C space. The sharp symbol changes the C natural to a C♯. Go up one half step from C♯ to D and that's the name of the key. Cross check this with one of the charts.

Let's try another one. The excerpt below has five sharps in the key signature. The farthest sharp to the right is on the second space up from the bottom, the A space. The sharp sign changes the A natural to an A♯. Go up one half step from A♯ to B and that's the name of the key. Again, cross check this with one of the charts.

There's a different rule for flat keys. First of all, you need at least two flats in the key signature for this rule to work. That's why you have to memorize that only one flat in a key signature means the key of F. Anyway, find the flat that's the farthest to the right and go back one flat to the left. Determine which line or space it's on and that will name the key.

The excerpt below has three flats in its key signature. The farthest flat to the right is on the second space up from the bottom, the A space. The next flat sign to the left of it is in the top space of the staff or the E space. The presence of this flat sign changes the E natural to an E♭ and since it's the second flat sign from the right, our key is E♭. So, whenever you see three flats in a key signature, the key is E♭.

Let's do one more for practice. The excerpt below has four flats in its key signature. The farthest flat to the right is on the fourth line up from the bottom, the D line, which changes all the Ds into D♭ notes. The next flat sign to the left of it is in the second space up from the bottom of the staff or the A space. The presence of this flat sign changes the A natural to an A♭ and since it's the second flat sign from the right, our key is A♭.

If you don't have a key signature or sheet music to look at, it's more difficult to determine a song's key. While there are exceptions, I look for the chord the song ends on or resolves to. More often than not, this will be the root or I chord of the key. So, if the last chord is a G, the song is more than likely in the key of G, etc. **Be forewarned, there are songs that don't adhere to this tendency, and we have to allow for minor keys.** (We'll get to minors later.) Still, I try to eliminate the "ends in G, must be G" possibility before considering any others.

Let's analyze and transpose another song, one with a few more chords. It's an old traditional American song entitled *Don't Let Your Deal Go Down*. If you're not familiar with it, never fear, it's pretty simple and the concepts we'll discuss will make sense whether you know the song or not. By the way, it's a good fun song. Reminds me of a joke: Skeleton walks into a bar and says, "Gimme a beer and a mop." The song is on the next two pages.

Don't Let Your Deal Go Down is written here in the key of G. How do we know that? The best way is to analyze the key signature by counting up the sharp or flat signs, apply the rules or consult one of the charts. We can also see that each eight measure section, verse and chorus, resolves to the G chord. If my rule of thumb is correct, G is more than likely the I chord and

Here are the chords that are derived from the G major scale.

(Key of G) G	Am	Bm	C	D	Em	F#°	G
I	ii	iii	IV	V	vi	vii	VIII/I

I can hear you already, "Whoa, just a New York minute there buddy! You said *Don't Let Your Deal Go Down* was in the key of G and it's got an E7, an A7, and a D7 in it. None of them are in that bunch of chords from the G major scale!" Right you are, go to the head of the class! As I mentioned before, these chords (I ii iii etc.) are built using only the **naturally occurring** notes of the G major scale and we can change them if we want. After all, we're musicians. Not only that, we're guitarists! We can do whatever the heck we want! (And in some cases we'll even get away with it!)

In the case of this tune, we're going to change the chords from minors to dominant seventh chords to accommodate the melody, which has

the song is in the key of G. Familiarize yourself with *Don't Let Your Deal Go Down*. Once you've done that, we'll work on transposing it to another key.

I've played through *Don't Let Your Deal Go Down* and have realized that I can sing it better in the key of D than as written in the key of G. How do I get from the key of G to the key of D? Well, obviously I could slap on the ol' capo and play the chords shown in the music. Where would I put the capo? Use the capo chart to figure it out.

How can I transpose *Don't Let Your Deal Go Down* without a capo? Let's start by analyzing the chords to the song in the key of G. We can see by examining the music that the chord progression is E7, A7, D7 and G and that this progression repeats throughout the song.

some notes (third measure C#, etc.) not in the G major scale. The chords will still be six and two chords, they'll just be dominant major chords and instead of using the lowercase Roman numerals which denote minor chords, we'll change them to upper case to reflect major chords. (Don't worry, the number system will still work no matter what the chord suffixes are as long as we keep them consistent. For example, if our ii chord is a minor seven in one key, it will be a minor seven in the key we transpose to. Just like with the capo exercises.)

This chord progression, E7 - A7 - D7 - G is known as a "VI - II - V - I" ("six - two - five - one") chord progression. To play *Don't Let Your Deal*

Don't Let Your Deal Go Down

Go Down in a different key, all we have to do is substitute VI, II, V, I chords from the new key for the VI, II, V, I chords of the original key of G. Look at the example below which we've changed to include dominant seventh chords instead of the naturally occurring minors.

(Key of G)	G	A7	B7	C7	D7	E7	F#°	G
	I	II	III	IV	V	VI	vii	VIII/I
(Key of D)	D	E7	F#7	G7	A7	B7	C#°	D

Our VI, II, V chord progression from the key of G (chords E7, A7, D7, G) will be changed to B7, E7, A7, D. Just like you did with our capo exercises, write in a B7 everywhere you see an E7 in the song, write in an E7 everywhere you see an A7, etc. Play through *Don't Let Your Deal Go Down* in both keys and listen for similarities and differences. Pay particular attention to how both chord progressions move in the same way.

It's important that you begin to think of a song's chords by their number and function within the key. While on a practical level you need to identify the B7 chord as the transposed E7 chord, it'll be much more useful in the long run if you think of them both as VI ("six") chords rather than the unrelated B7 or E7. Same with thinking of the E7 in the key of D and the A7 in the key of G as II ("two") chords. It's also important to keep the contexts of chords within a key straight because with-out them, the numbers are meaningless. For example, an E7 is not always a VI chord. It's only a VI relative to the key of G. Relative to the key of D the E7 is a II chord. Relative to the key of A the E7 is a V chord. Eventually you'll be able to hear a chord progression and identify the relative changes in your head as a I-IV-V or a I-vi-ii-V-I, etc. and be able to place them in any key.

The chart below summarizes all this theory and shows the keys with their naturally occurring chords. It's very similar to the capo and scale charts you've already worked with. To use it, find the horizontal line showing the key of the song you want to transpose. Identify which columns, I, ii, iii, IV, V, etc. the known chords fall in. Then, simply read up or down to the new key and find the transposed chords. Remember that you can change the chords shown below to majors and sevenths as your situation demands it, just like we did with *Don't Let Your Deal Go Down*.

Scale and Chord Chart

Key	-	Scale / Chord	1 / I	2 / ii	3 / iii	4 / IV	5 / V	6 / vi	7 / vii	8 (1) / VIII (I)
C	none		C	Dm	Em	F	G	Am	B°	C
F	1 - ♭		F	Gm	Am	B♭	C	Dm	E°	F
B♭	2 - ♭		B♭	Cm	Dm	E♭	F	Gm	A°	B♭
E♭	3 - ♭		E♭	Fm	Gm	A♭	B♭	Cm	D°	E♭
A♭	4 - ♭		A♭	B♭m	Cm	D♭	E♭	Fm	G°	A♭
D♭	5 - ♭		D♭	E♭m	Fm	G♭	A♭	B♭m	C°	D♭
G♭	6 - ♭		G♭	A♭m	B♭m	C♭	D♭	E♭m	F°	G♭
C♭	7 - ♭		C♭	D♭m	E♭m	F♭	G♭	A♭m	B♭°	C♭
C♯	7 - ♯		C♯	D♯m	E♯m	F♯	G♯	A♯m	B♯°	C♯
F♯	6 - ♯		F♯	G♯m	A♯m	B	C♯	D♯m	E♯°	F♯
B	5 - ♯		B	C♯m	D♯m	E	F♯	G♯m	A♯°	B
E	4 - ♯		E	F♯m	G♯m	A	B	C♯m	D♯°	E
A	3 - ♯		A	Bm	C♯m	D	E	F♯m	G♯°	A
D	2 - ♯		D	Em	F♯m	G	A	Bm	C♯°	D
G	1 - ♯		G	Am	Bm	C	D	Em	F♯°	G

Let's use the chart to transpose another song. It's a beautiful old ballad, a favorite of mine entitled *Fair and Tender Ladies*. I usually sing the song as written below, in a key that accommodates a typical male voice. Let's transpose it to accommodate a typical female voice.

When we discussed this type of male to female transposition in the capo section of this book, I mentioned that I usually start with the capo on the fifth or seventh fret and then move up or down from there depending upon the individual's vocal range. We're going to do the same type of thing here. It turns out that when we capo up five frets on the guitar, we're raising the pitch of the chords or melody we're playing by an interval of a fourth or two and one half steps. When we capo up seven frets, we're raising the pitch of what we play by an interval of a fifth or three and one half steps. Let's see if we can do these transpositions without the capo.

First look at the music on the next page, play through it to familiarize yourself with the melody, chords, and lyrics, and determine what key the song is in. You know a few ways to do this but let's take the most fool proof and look at the song's key signature. Do you see any sharps or flats between the treble clef sign and the time signature? That tells us that the song is in the key of C.

Now analyze the chords with the help of the Scale and Chord Chart on the previous page and determine the Roman numerals for each of them. Remember to stay in the context of the key of C as you proceed. First find the key of C row in the chart. Follow over to the right and find the song's first chord, a C. The C chord is in the "I" or "one" column. Pencil in a "I" by every C chord in *Fair and Tender Ladies*. Next find the G in the same key of C row. It's in the "V" or "five" column. Write a "V"

by every G in the music. Now find the Dm chord in the same row. It's in the "ii" or "two" column. Write a "ii" by every Dm chord. We now know that the chord progression to the first few measures of *Fair and Tender Ladies* could be described as "I-V-ii-I" or "one-five-two-one." After that it's "I-ii-V-I" or "one-two-five-one."

Now that we know the chord numbers of *Fair and Tender Ladies*, we need to transpose the whole song up by an interval of a fourth. How can we find out what that new key will be? Look at the key of C row in the chart. Intervals are easy to figure out. In the context of both scales and chords in keys, the interval between the first and second note or chord is a **second**, the interval between the first and the third is a **third**, the interval between the first and the fourth is a **fourth**, and so on. In this case we want to find out what key is an interval of a fourth above the key of C. If we start at the I chord of the key of C, which is a C, and move to the right to the IV column, we'll see an F. That tell us that we want to transpose *Fair and Tender Ladies* to the key of F, which is a fourth above C. Now it's just a question of swapping the "I-V-ii-I" chords of C for the "I-V-ii-I" of F.

Find the I chord in the key of C row. It's in the I column. Follow down to the key of F row and you'll see that the I chord in the key of F is an F. Write an F in the music wherever there's a C chord or the "I" that you already added. Now find the G chord in the key of C row. It's in the "V" column. Follow down to the key of F row and you'll see that the V chord in the key of F is a C chord. Write a C in wherever you find a G or V in your music. Finally, locate the Dm chord in the key of C row. It's in the "ii" column. Follow that down to the key of F row and you'll find and Gm chord. As before, write in Gm wherever you see a Dm or "ii" in

Fair and Tender Ladies

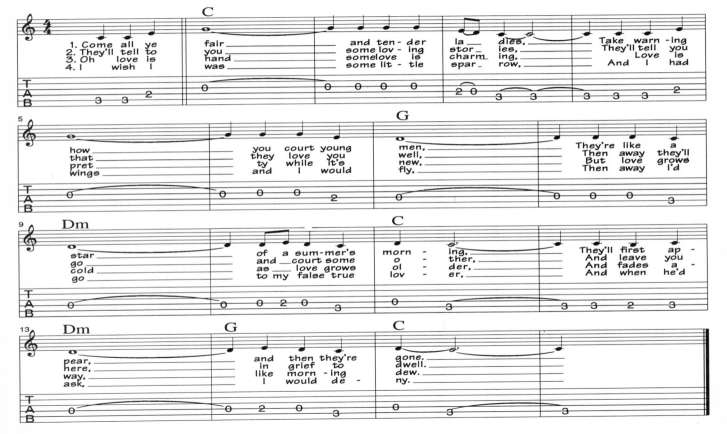

your music. That's all there is to it. You just transposed *Fair and Tender Ladies* from the key of C to the key of F, without a capo.

Now it may be that the key of F is still too low for our singer. What would be the next logical thing to try? How about transposing the song even higher to the key of G? The key of G would be an interval of a fifth above the key of C, an interval of a major second above the key of F. Use the chart the same way and transpose from the key of F to the key of G. All you have to do is find the key of F chords in their respective Roman numeral columns and follow down to the new key of G. Write the new chords in your music.

How about one more exercise with *Fair and Tender Ladies*? Our female singer just got a better gig so she sends a sub. Turns out he's a male singer, a tenor. He can sing higher than I can but not as high as our female singer. So instead of my original key of C arrangement, we need to try the song in the key of D or E. Luckily, you know what to do. Start from the original key of C or from one of the transposed keys, find the I,

ii, and V columns and follow up or down to each new key to find the new chords. Simple as pie! Speaking of pies and eating, remember the one about the two cannibals? They're eating a clown and one says to the other "Does this taste funny to you?"

We should also briefly discuss minor keys. For the most part they'll work about the same as major keys, at least regarding transposing and the use of capos. There are a few varieties of minor keys with different qualities but for the purposes our discussions of keys and key signatures, we'll look mostly at the natural minor.

As you've learned, every key signature describes a unique major key. But it also describes that major key's relative minor. The relative minor scale, also called the natural minor, is built on the sixth tone of the major scale. It uses the same notes as the relative major scale and thus shares its key signature. In the key of C the sixth tone of the major scale is A. The A natural minor scale is as follows:

A		B		C		D		E		F		G		A
1		2		3		4		5		6		7		8
	wh		1/2		wh		wh		1/2		wh		wh	

As with the major scale, chords are built on each of these notes.

	Am	Bm	C	D	Em	F$\sharp^{\circ}$	G	Am
Chord #	i	ii	III	IV	v	vi$^{\circ}$	VII	viii/i

It gets a little confusing here as music history intervenes to change what's a very clear and predictable system. As you can see in the A minor chart above, the five chord is Em. Unfortunately that Em is a pretty weak chord and doesn't act as dominant as a V in a major key. So, the powers that be decided to change it from an E minor to an E major chord so that it would lead the ear back to the Am. So, if you find a piece written in Am, it will probably have an E or E7 in place of the Em. We won't get much deeper into theory as it's well beyond the scope of this QwikGuide™. Suffice it to say that every major scale has a relative minor built on the sixth note of the scale. The key signature of the major key can also describe the relative minor key.

Here's a great old song in a minor key, *Joshua Fought the Battle of Jericho*. Let's transpose it to a couple of other keys.

Joshua Fought the Battle of Jericho

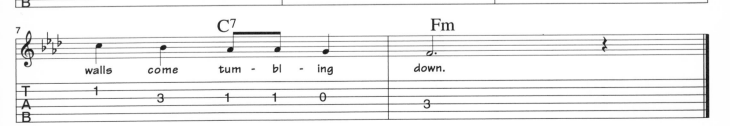

First determine what key the song is in. Since it begins and ends with minor chords, it's a good bet that it's in a minor key! Looking at those chords we see an Fm chord so it's reasonable to assume that *Joshua Fought the Battle of Jericho* is in the key of F minor. How can we be sure? Check the key signature. As you can see, it has four flats. We can either look four flats up on the chart or use our rule of thumb to find the last flat to the right, go back one, and see that our key is A♭. But wait a minute, didn't I just say that the key was probably F minor? What gives? Well, we said that a key signature defines both a major key and its relative minor, which is built on the sixth note of the major scale. If you check the chart, you'll see that F is the sixth of the A♭ scale making F minor the relative minor of the key of A♭. So it all makes sense, *Joshua Fought the Battle of Jericho* is in F minor.

Let's transpose *Joshua Fought the Battle of Jericho* to both G minor and C minor. There are a couple of ways to go about it. One is to use the chart without regard to the numbers of chords in their respective keys. To do that, all you have to do is find any F on the chart and move up or down the column to any G, which is the first key we'll transpose to. Since the original chord is an Fm, the transposed chords must match it in quality and the new chord is Gm. Now go back to the row the F was in and follow over to the C column. Then move up or down the same number of spaces you traveled to find the Fm to Gm transposition and you'll find a D. Since the original chord was a C7, the transposed chord needs to match it in quality so it'll be a D7.

You could also use the chart to find the Fm in the sixth column of the key of A♭ row. Now, staying in the sixth column, move up to the Gm. Do the same move with the C7, even though you don't have a C7 on the chart. Move up to the same row you just found the Gm in and there you'll see a Dm. Since the original chord was a C7, the transposed chord needs to be a D7.

As you work through exercises like these, you'll gradually memorize the numbers of chords in every key. At this point it can seem like a daunting and confusing task. But if you start analyzing chord progressions right now and work through transposing you'll be amazed at how quickly it will all come together. It also helps to start with relatively simple two or three chord songs. Once you can recognize these simple chord progressions like I-V-I, I-IV-V-I, I-vi-ii-V, etc., you'll begin to hear them in millions of pop, rock, folk, and jazz songs.

Answers to Quiz on page 24

1. Sixth fret.
2. E, B, G, D, A, E.
3. a) G#/A♭, b) C, c) A, d) D, e) C, f) A#/B♭.
4. Capo fret one/play in the key of E; Capo fret five / play in the key of C.
5. a) Two, b) one.
6. What.
7. C#/D♭.
8. That answer, my friend, is blowing in the wind.

The Nashville Numbering System

By now you should have a pretty good idea how to transpose with and without the capo. You've also analyzed a few songs and determined their keys and the Roman numerals of their accompaniment chords relative to that key. You'll put this knowledge to use in our examination of The Nashville Numbering System.

The Nashville Numbering System uses the same basic concepts and music theory you've already worked with. The main difference is that most Nashville-style chord charts use Arabic numerals instead of Roman numerals to identify a chord in a key. And, there's no 100% accepted standard for writing a Nashville Numbering chart. You're likely to find a range of variations which may include anything from standard music notation symbols to something the arranger invents. We'll look at some of the most common styles. Again, numbered chord systems are not limited to Nashville sessions or country music. Since they use traditional music theory, you'll find variations of the system in all types of music from classical to jazz to country to rock.

Why do we use The Nashville Numbering System? Because it's a quick and easy way to describe a song, a chord progression, even an arrangement to musicians. It's a language that's understood all over the world by musicians of all styles. And, a musician need not read music to understand and perform a Nashville Numbering System chord chart. These types of charts are especially helpful when musicians play a part they improvise rather than one that's written out completely in stan-

dard music notation. This is the way much of the pop, rock, and country music of today is performed and recorded. The Nashville Numbering chart gives all the musicians a place to start, whether they read music or not. Of course standard music notation is still very important and indispensable for many applications including horn or string sections.

One of the greatest advantages of a numbering system chart is that it is not tied to any key. Suppose an arranger prepares a song for a studio session with a Nashville Numbering chart in the key of D. Now suppose that the singer decides at the session that he needs to sing the song in the key of E. Without having to rewrite ten charts, the producer simply tells the musicians that the key is E, not D. The players simply adjust the context from D to E.

The Nashville Numbering System also comes in handy when two guitarists might need to capo at different frets. Let's say our singer wants one guitar to play beefy chords out of open E while the other capos up and lightly fingerpicks a simple pattern. You already know about the possible choices from your experimentation with the capo. The second guitarist decides to capo at the fourth fret and fingerpick out of the key of C. The cool thing here is that both guitarists can read the same Nashville Numbering chart and interpret it differently depending upon the key they are in.

So, what does a Nashville Numbering chart look like? As I mentioned, I've seen a wide variation of styles but all of them draw on the basic

46

music theory that you've studied so far. You'll see several styles and sizes in the next few pages. Most use Arabic numerals (1, 3m, 5) rather than Roman numerals (I, iii, V). Let's look at a few typical charts and analyze what makes them tick. But first… A traveling salesman knocks on a farmhouse door. Getting no answer he walks around to the back yard where he finds the farmer feeding a pig, but not in the usual way. Instead, the farmer is holding the pig under his arm and lifting it up to apples on a tree. The farmer holds the pig while it eats one apple to the core and then moves the pig on to the next apple. The salesman watches the pig eat three or four apples and then can't help but interrupt the farmer. "Wouldn't it save some time if you shook down a bunch of apples and let the pig eat them off the ground?" The farmer looks at the salesman in disbelief and says, "What's time to a pig?" Now where was I? Oh yeah, a simple Nashville Numbering chart.

In the next column you'll find a simple Nashville Numbering chart to the Mexican folk song *La Bamba*. The vertical lines represent measures, four beats per measure, and there are generally four measures across the page to help the reader keep track of where the song is going. The double vertical lines at the beginning and end of the verse and chorus mimic the double bars used in standard notation to delineate parts.

It should be obvious that *La Bamba* is basically a "1, 4, 5" ("one, four, five") song. So what chords should you play in the key of F? All you have to do is figure out what the one, four, and five of the key of F are. If my calculations are correct, the chords in F would be F, B♭, and C7. Now, quick like a bunny, play the same thing in the key of G. Easy, huh? Well, maybe not quite yet, but the process of transposing in this way will make it easier the more you practice. Now try the key of D. How about C?

Key of F
Intro/pickup/one bar at beginning
Verse:
|| 1 4 | 5 | 1 4 | 5 |
| 1 4 | 5 | 1 4 | 5 | 1 4 | 5 ||
Chorus:
|| 1 4 | 5 | 1 4 | 5 |
| 1 4 | 5 | 1 4 | 5 ||

Number Chart #1: "La Bamba"

Depending upon the style of whoever is writing out the chart, it may contain more or less information on the specifics of playing the charted song. It may indicate a time signature, like 3/4, 2/4, or 4/4, like the above. It may include chord suffixes, bass line or rhythmic info.

Let's look at another style of chart, this time with boxes to indicate measures and chart out a song you've already worked with *Fair and Tender Ladies*. These are often called "box charts."

This chart looks pretty much the same as the previous one with a couple of differences. First of all, the chords are all in boxes which represent one measure. This really makes it easy to follow and keep your place in the song. This symbol ╱ means to repeat the previous measure. "2-" means to play the two minor chord. If we were using Roman numerals instead of Arabic, we'd use upper case for major and lower case for minor. In this system a minor chord is shown with either a minus or a small case "m." Any other chord suffix can be added to a number and generally they're the same as you'd find in the chord name itself. For example, 7, 6, augmented or plus, dim or diminished (noted with the degree symbol °), major seven or (noted with a triangle sym-

bol), 9, 11, suspended, and so on. You can also expect to see just about any other musical symbol or term incorporated into the chart from rests to fermatas. Be sure that you work on playing *Fair and Tender Ladies* in a variety of keys.

| 1 | ℅ | ℅ | ℅ |

| ℅ | ℅ | 5 | ℅ |

| 2- | ℅ | 1 | ℅ |

| 2- | 5 | 1 | ℅ |

Box Chart #2
("Fair and Tender Ladies")

The examples you've seen so far are quite simple because they represent simple songs. As the music and arrangements get more complex, so do the charts. Here's one that features a chord progression that hundreds of 1950s rock ballads used. It's usually re-

ferred to as a "one-six-four-five" even though it has other passages as well in the full arrangement shown. Play through it in the key of C. Try to figure out the chords in your head. If you get stuck, consult the chart.

Intro:

$$||16- \ |\ 45\ |\ 16- \ |\ 45\ ||$$

Verse:

$$||:16- \ |\ 41\ |\ 16- \ |\ 45\ |\ 4\ |14|\ 14\ |\ 15:||$$

Chorus:

$$||45\ |\ 16- \ |\ 45\ |\ 6- \ |45\ |\ 16- \ |\ 4\ |\ 5||$$

Verse:

$$||16- \ |\ 41\ |\ 16- \ |\ 45\ |\ 4\ |14|\ 14\ |\ 15\ ||$$

Solo:

$$||16- \ |\ 45\ |\ 16- \ |\ 45\ ||$$

Chorus:

$$||45\ |\ 16- \ |\ 45\ |\ 6- \ |45\ |\ 16- \ |\ 4\ |\ 5||$$

Verse plus ending:

$$||16- \ |\ 41\ |\ 16- \ |\ 45\ |\ 4\ |14|\ 14\ |\ 15\ |$$
$$|\ 15\ |\ 1\ ||$$

Number Chart #3: "'50s Rock"

The song has several sections including an introduction, a verse, chorus, solo (which is over the changes of the introduction), and a verse

plus ending. Measures are noted by the vertical lines and every measure has two chords in it. Each chord is played for only two beats. Again, the double vertical lines delineate sections of the song. Try playing through it in the keys of F, G, C, etc.

Nashville charts often don't include boxes or even measure lines. It can get confusing and you may have to figure out the meter (how many beats per measure) when you play the song through the first time. Below is an example of a chart made for the traditional song *Amazing Grace* that has no measure markings. If you've never heard the song you might not know that it's in 3/4 time. Typical charts may or may not include that information. In this case each number or repetition represents one 3/4 measure.

Intro:

$$||1\ 5\ 1\ 1\ ||$$

Verse:

$$||: 1\ 1\ 4\ 11\ 1\ 5\ 5\ 1\ 1\ 4\ 16m\ 5\ 4\ 1\ :||$$

Outro:

$$||1\ 5\ 1\ 1\ ||$$

Number Chart #4: "Amazing Grace"

After the intro, the song repeats on the verse. The chart may or may not say how many times to repeat the verse. Solos may be added which will extend the form. You have to ask or listen. After the vocal and solo sections, the song ends with an "outro." While I'm not sure that "outro" is an official word in Webster's, any musician will know what you mean. Play *Amazing Grace* in as many keys as you can think of and then compare what you played to the following arrangement. Reminds me of a story. A bear walks over to a driveup window and says, "Gimme a ....hamburger." Clerk asks, "Why the big pause." (This is an audio story. You may have to read it aloud a few times to gain the maximum groan effect.)

Let's add a few variations to the basic *Amazing Grace* chart. We'll incorporate some other symbols you might encounter in a typical Nashville Numbering System chart. The result is in the right hand column.

The first thing you'll see at the top of the chart are the words "Keys of D and E. 3/4 time." How can a song be in two keys at once? It can't. However, from reading that line we know that there are two different keys involved with this song. We also know that it's in 3/4 or waltz time and that each measure will have three beats in it.

Moving on down the page we see that the first section is an intro. Once again the measures and chord changes aren't divided by vertical lines or placed in boxes. Each number will be played for three beats unless the measure is subdivided. The intro is four measures long. The fourth "1" chord has a diamond around it. This means to play the first beat of the measure and let it ring for two more beats.

Next is the verse section. Again it's enclosed in double bars with a repeat sign or colon. That means that you should read the changes straight down until you reach the second repeat sign. At that point you'll go back to the first repeat mark or colon and play the changes again, skip the first ending (noted with a circled "1") and proceed to the second ending. The form should be pretty clear at this point but there are

Keys of D and E. 3/4 time

Intro:
‖1 5 1 ◇1◇‖

Verse:
‖: 1 $\frac{1}{3}$ 4 1

1 6m 2m 5

① 1 $\frac{1}{3}$ 4 1

6m 5 4 1̇ :‖

② 6m 5 1 6̇^{7} ‖   mod

Key of E
Verse:
‖ 1 $\frac{1}{3}$ 4 1

1 6m 2m 5

1 $\frac{1}{3}$ 4 1

6m 5 4 1 ‖

Outro:
‖1/$\frac{1}{7}$/6m   5/5^7/ 5$^{7\,sus}$ 1 ◇1◇‖

still a few things inside the verse that we need to look at.

In the first line of the verse we find what looks like a fraction, $\frac{1}{3}$. The top number ("1") tells us what chord to play and the bottom number ("3") specifies the bass note played with the chord. Our one chord is a D and the bass note would be the third note of the D scale or F♯. Depending upon what the arranger wants, this may apply to you or only the bass player.

In the second line of the verse you'll see the familiar "6m" and "2m." Remember that we could have also used the minus sign ("-") to signify minor chords.

The fourth line is the first ending of the verse. You'll notice a period above the last chord, which is a 1. A period above a chord means to play only the first beat of the measure and not let the chord ring over the other two beats. It's a stop. After it you see the repeat sign that tells you to go back to the beginning of the verse.

The second ending, which is the fifth line of the verse has a couple of new things as well. The last chord has both a 7 after it and a period above it. The period means that same thing it meant in the first ending. The seven means to play the chord as a dominant. In the key of D this would be what? You are correct, a B7! After that you'll see the word "mod." Generally that means to stop what you're doing, change into bell bottoms, granny glasses, tie dyed T-shirt, slather yourself in patchouli oil, start speaking with a British accent, and become thoroughly annoying. But in this context "mod" stands for **modulation**. A modulation is when a song changes keys. Ah! That's how a song can be in two keys, just not two keys at the same time. So, we're modulating from the key of D to the key of E. The last chord we play in the key of D is the dominant sixth or B7. But the B7 is also the five of the key of E so it's a pivotal chord that moves us to the new key.

Now we come to the verse in the new key of E and the chord numbers should now be thought of in that context. The form of this verse is exactly like the previous with a couple of minor exceptions. First, there are no first and second endings, just the fourth line which is essentially the first ending, and the last chord of the part, a 1, is given three full beats without the stop.

Last we come to the outro. What the heck is going on here? The slashes split the 3/4 measure into three beats and we need to play a different chord on every beat. On the first beat you just play the one chord. The "fraction" on beat two that looks like "one seventh" means to play the one chord with the seventh note of the scale in the bass. In the key of E that bass note is D♯. The last beat of that measure has a six minor chord. Going on to the next measure we find that beat one has a simple five chord, beat two has a five dominant chord, and beat three has a five dominant with a suspended fourth note added. When you see "sus" you need to raise the third of the chord by one half step. The notes of the B7 chord are B, D♯, F♯, and A. So here you raise the D♯ to an E.

The penultimate measure resolves to the one. The last measure is also on the one but the diamond tells us that we only strum beat one. The fermata (a.k.a. "bird's eye") above the diamond tells us to hold the last note and let it ring beyond the end of the measure. The producer or band leader will usually direct the band when to end the hold.

There's a lot of information in this *Amazing Grace* chord chart. The first challenge is to play it as written in the keys of D and E. Of course as soon as you figure that out you should move on to other sets of keys like G and A, C and D, F and G, and all the rest. It may be difficult for you and I have to admit that it's sometimes difficult for me to figure out some of the transpositions. But working through them in this way is the only way to learn them. It can sometimes be a struggle, but once you have that working knowledge of the system in your head, you'll never lose it.

Be prepared for the many style variations in number charts. Most won't include near the detail that this one has. Some will have vertical lines between measures. Others will use the fraction nomenclature. Expect to see symbols that you've never see before!

Before we wind this enterprise up, here are a few Nashville Number Style charts to various well-known songs. Read through them in different keys and try to figure out what song they are. It won't matter if you know the songs or not. Approach them as though you are reading them for the first time at a recording session with no additional information. I'll give you some general hints regarding titles. I can't tell you the names of the songs or "the man" will come and get me. And believe you me, you do NOT want to spend any time in copyright prison!

The chart in the next column is based on an old folk / blues standard. In the mid-sixties it was a huge hit for a British rock group. I transcribed the Doc Watson recording of it for my *Doc Watson and Clarence Ashley* book (Mel Bay MB97056). The key and meter are both shown. Though there are no repeat marks, you'll play the chords of the first four lines as many times as necessary. The last time through the piece, substitute the measure labeled "last time" for the 3^7 chord shown in the form and under the line.

Number Chart #6:
"House of the Rising Sun"

Key of C. 6/8 time

	6-	1	2	4
6-	1	3	3^7
6-	1	2	4
6-	3^7	6-	3^7 || last time	6-	

Here are the changes to a swing tune made world famous by a great 1930s string duo. It's written here in the key of Am but lots of people play it in the key of Dm. Try it in every minor key you can think of.

Key of Am

	1-	1-	4-	4-
5	5	1-	1^7
4-	4-	1-	1-
5	5	1-	1-	

Number Chart #7

Next is a great standard with a state's name in its title. You can listen to the same chord changes and play solos all night long (we'll be your band!) to a similar tune on my *BackUP TRAX: Swing & Jazz* book and CD set (Mel Bay MB94344BCD).

Key of F. Form: AABA

Intro:

||1 6^7 | 2m 5^7 | 1 6m | 2m 5^7||

Part A:

||: 1 | 3^7 | 6m 1^7 | 4 4m |
|1 6^7| 2m 5^7 |①3m 6^7 | 2m 5^7 :|
②|1 4 | 1 3^7 ||

Bridge (B):

|6m 2m | 6m 4^7| 6m 2m | 6m 2^7 |
|6m 2m | 6m 7^7 | 3m 6^7 | 2m 5^7 ||

Repeat of part A:

|| 1 | 3^7 | 6m 1^7 | 4 4m |
|1 6^7| 2m 5^7 | 1 6^7| 2m 5^7||

Last 4 bars last time:

|1 6^7| 2m 5^7 | 1 4 | 1 ||

Number Chart #8

This chart tells us the key of the piece and the form of the performance, AABA. This is a typical pop song form where the first eight measures ("A") are played twice (hence the repeat sign and first and second endings), the middle eight measures ("B" also called the bridge) are played once, and the first eight ("A") are repeated. The song would usually be played through several times. On the last time through, plug in the four measures marked "Last 4 bars last time" instead of the last four measures of the repeated "A" part.

Chart #9 has the chord changes to a beautiful love song written and recorded in the late 1960s by another British band.

In the intro, play the first measure as directed and let the second chord ring. Play the chord in measure two and let it ring. The tempo will begin in measure three of the intro. Part A sails along predictably until the first ending. The slashes under the chords mean that the first is given two beats and the other two are given one beat each. Then the piece modulates from the key of G to the key of B♭. The ♭7^7 chord in the key of G is also the 5^7 chord in the key of B♭. It's a pivotal chord that makes the modulation work smoothly. Remember that the numbers in Part B should all be thought of in the context of the new key, which is B♭. At the end of Part B, the piece modulates again, back to the key of G, making use of another pivot chord, 3^7. In the last measure of the ending, you'll strum the 1 chord once and let it ring.

Chart #10 is a great jam tune that everybody from country to jazz pickers love to play by the hour. You can listen to the same chord changes and play solos all night long (we'll be your band!) to a similar tune on my *BackUP TRAX: Swing & Jazz* book and CD set (Mel Bay MB94344BCD).

Key of G

Intro, time as directed:

$$\|1 \langle \widehat{3} \rangle \, \langle \flat \widehat{3} \rangle \mid 2{-}^7 \; 5^7 \|$$

Part A:

$$\|: 1 \;\; 2{-} \mid 3{-} \;\; 4 \mid 1 \;\; 2{-} \mid 3{-} \;\; 4 \mid$$

$$|7{-} \;\; 3^7| \;\; / \!\!/ \;\; |6{-} \;\; 2{-} \;|^{①} \overline{2{-}^7 \;\; 5^7} :\|^{②} \overline{2{-}^7 \;\; 5 \;\; \flat 7^7} \;\| \quad \text{Modulate to B}\flat$$

Part B:

$$\|1 \;\; 6{-} \mid 2{-} \;\; 3^7 \mid 6{-} \qquad \mid 2{-} \;\; 3^7 \;\| \quad \text{Modulate to G}$$

Part A:

$$\| 1 \;\; 2{-} \mid 3{-} \;\; 4 \mid 1 \;\; 2{-} \mid 3{-} \;\; 4 \mid$$

$$|7{-} \;\; 3 \mid \;\; / \!\!/ \;\; |6{-} \;\; 2{-} \mid 2^7 \;\; 5^7 \|$$

Ending:

$$\| 1 \;\; 2{-} \mid 3{-} \;\; 4 \mid 1 \;\; 2{-} \mid 3{-} \;\; 4 \mid \langle \widehat{1} \rangle \;\|$$

Number Chart #9

Key of A♭

Intro:

$$\| 6{-} \;\; 3^7 \mid 6{-} \;\; 3^7 \mid 1^7 \;\; 7^7 \mid \flat 7^7 \; 6^7 \mid 2^7 \; 5^7 \mid 1 \;\|$$

$$\| 6^7 \mid / \!\!/ \mid / \!\!/ \mid / \!\!/ \mid$$
$$| 2^7 \mid / \!\!/ \mid / \!\!/ \mid / \!\!/ \mid$$
$$| 5^7 \mid / \!\!/ \mid / \!\!/ \mid / \!\!/ \mid$$
$$| 1 \mid 2^7 \; 5^7 \mid 1 \mid 3^7 \|$$

$$\| 6^7 \mid / \!\!/ \mid / \!\!/ \mid / \!\!/ \mid$$
$$| 2^7 \mid / \!\!/ \mid / \!\!/ \mid / \!\!/ \|$$

$$\| 6{-} \;\; 3^7 \mid 6{-} \;\; 3^7 \mid 1^7 \;\; 7^7 \mid \flat 7^7 \; 6^7 \mid 2^7 \; 5^7 \mid 1 \;\|$$

Number Chart #10

Chart #11 is a doozy! It's such a doozy in fact that I'm going to give it to you twice. The first chart is written in the typical style where all the chords are listed relative to the key the song starts out in. It gets a little thick because it modulates to several different keys in the course of the form. So, the second chart (#12) shows the modulations and each new section needs to be thought of in the context of its new key. I find the second chart to be much more informative, especially if I'm going to solo over the changes. I see exactly what key I'm in and the changes make more sense. There are also some nice arrangement moves that we'll discuss later.

You may need to pencil in the actual chords to really understand all the changes that are going on in the song. True, this is a difficult song, but it's played by all kinds of musicians all over the world. It's not out of the ordinary at all and it's very likely that you'll come across something this involved in a studio. By the way, it's a pop standard that was a huge hit for a very famous electric guitar player and electronic innovator and his partner in the 1950s. Take a gander.

In both arrangements the intro has a distinctive rhythmic twist. The first chord is a 3m7 with a dot over it. The dot means to play the chord on beat one and rest through the first three beats of the next measure. On the fourth beat of measure two there's another 3m with this symbol before it: >. This means to play the chord on the "and" of beat three to anticipate the chord. This pattern continues through the intro. At the end of the intro you play a five seven chord on beat one and let it ring through both measures.

In the "Tune" part of the song, the first chord has a little triangle and a seven after it. That signifies a major seven chord. In the fifth mea-

Key of G. Intro:

$$\| \ 3\dot{m}^7 \ | \ \{\{\{ \ >3m^7 \ | \ \flat3\dot{m}^7 \ | \ \{\{\{ >\flat3^7m \ |$$

$$| \ 2\dot{m}^7 \ | \ \{\{\{ \ >2m \ | \langle 5^7 \rangle | \langle 5^7 \rangle \ \|$$

Tune:

$$\|: \ 1^{\triangle 7} \ | \ \% \ | \ 1m^7 \ | \ 4^7 \ | \ \flat7^{\triangle 7} \ | \ \% \ | \ \flat7m^7 \ | \ \flat3^7 \ |$$

$$| \ \flat6^{\triangle 7} \ | \ 2m^7 \ 5^{7\flat 9} \ \overline{ |^{①} 1m \ | \ 2m^7 \ 5^7 \ | \ 1^{\triangle 7} \ | \ 2m^7 \ 5^7 \ |}$$

$$\overline{| \ 3m^7 \ \flat3m^7 \ | \ 2m^7 \ 5^7 {:} \| }$$

$$\overline{^{②} | \ 1^{\triangle 7} \ | \ 2m^7 5^7 \ | \ 1^{\triangle 7} \ | \ 2m^7 \ 5^7 \ |}$$

$$\overline{| \ 3m \ \flat3m \ | \ 2m^7 \ 5^7 | \ 1 \ | \ \% \ \|}$$

* Last X to ending

Ending:

$$\|: \ 3m \ \flat3m \ | \ 2\dot{m} {:} \| \ _{3 \, X}$$

$$| \langle 1^{\triangle 7} \rangle \langle 1^{\triangle 7} \rangle \ \|$$

Key of G. Intro:

$$\| \ 3\dot{m}^7 \ | \ \gtrless\gtrless >3m^7 | \ \flat 3\dot{m}^7 \ | \ \gtrless\gtrless >\flat 3m^7 |$$

$$| \ 2\dot{m}^7 \ | \ \gtrless\gtrless >2m \ |\diamond 5^7|\diamond 5^7\diamond \ \|$$

Tune:

Mod key of F   Mod key of E♭

$$\|: \ 1^{\triangle 7}| \ \text{.⁄.} \ | \ 2m^7 | \ 5^7 | \ 1^{\triangle 7}| \ \text{.⁄.} \ | \ 2m^7| \ 5^7|$$

Mod key of Gm ①——— Mod key of G

$$|1m| \ 2m^7 \ 5^{7\flat 9}| \ 1m \ | \ 2m^7 \ 5^7 \ | \ 1^{\triangle 7}| \ 2m^7 \ 5^7|$$

$$| \ 3m \ \ \flat 3m \ \ | \ 2m^7 \ 5^7 :\|$$

② Mod key of G

$$| \ 1^{\triangle 7}| \ 2m^7 5^7 | \ 1^{\triangle 7}| \ 2m^7 \ 5^7 \ |$$

* Last X to ending

$$| \ 3m^7 \ \flat 3m \ ^7| \ 2m^7 \ 5^7| \ 1 \ | \ \text{.⁄.} \ \|$$

Ending:

$$\|: \ 3m^7 \ \flat 3m \ ^7 \ | \ 2\dot{m}^7:\| \ _{3\,X}$$

$$|\diamond 1^{\triangle 7}| \ 1^{\triangle 7}\diamond \ \|$$

Number Chart #12

sure there's a ♭7 ("flat seven") major seven. In the key of G, the seventh chord is an F♯ diminished. If you flat that you get an F natural chord, which will be played as a major seven or F major seven. Remember, the chord numbers in this arrangement are all in the context of the original key. In measure ten there's a five dominant chord with a flatted nine note ($5^{7\flat 9}$). Next is the first ending, a repeat of the first ten bars of the tune, then on to the second ending.

On the last time through the song, substitute the ending for the last four bars of the second ending. The first two bars of the ending repeat three times with a stop on the two minor chord each time. In the last two bars of the ending play a one major seven chord on beat one and let it ring over both measures.

The only difference between these two charts is that the modulations are noted in the second. You have to adjust your thinking to place the chord numbers in the context of each new key, and there are several, that the tune moves through. Which of the charts do **you** find easier to read and understand?

Acknowledgements

Thanks to my brigade of friends who helped me shape and mold this book. Special thanks to Bob Bergman, Carmen Burnett, Gene Tortora, Laura Alber and Charlotte Gibb for their corrections and suggestions; and to Jim Nunally for providing me with the guitar diagrams.

Coda

Your ultimate goal, as I mentioned above, is to train yourself to think of chords by their numerical designations, not their alphabetical names. This will allow you to put theory into practice as you begin to understand the relationships between chords and keys. You'll also find it easier to communicate with other musicians and open yourself up to wonderful unknown worlds of music. Most pop, folk, country, rock, and jazz songs tend to follow one of a handful of standard chord progressions. Musicians can indicate these quickly, clearly, and easily in one phrase like "one, five", "one, five, one, four, one, five, one," or "one, six, two, five." You'll also find that numbers like "one, six, two, five," shouted across a stage will be much more easily understood than the sound-alikes "Geeeee!, Eeeeee!, Aaaaay!, Deeeee!"

If you haven't done so already, look back at the songs in this book and write out Nashville Numbering System charts for each. Do the same with a variety of songs you already know. Make it a part of your daily practice to convert a few songs from your favorite songbook to number charts. If you're really ambitious, arrange a few with moves like those in *Amazing Grace*.

I agree, it's a lot to learn, and it'll be easier if you get a handle on how you're going to learn the whole system. In addition to making charts, I suggest that you work on learning the I and V chords in all keys. Pick a song or two or three, probably simple songs with only those two chords and move them through all the keys. Give yourself as much time as you need, weeks or months, to learn the Is and Vs. Next try a few songs with I, IV, and V chords, like *La Bamba*, and work them through the keys. After you've mastered I, IV and V, move on to songs with more changes like I, vi, ii, V or I, VI, II, V, etc. As you're working on these exercises, be sure to move the charts in this book through all the keys.

Give yourself time to understand these concepts. A short session of practice everyday will probably do more good than one marathon per week as you train your head and hands. The more you practice, the more you'll learn and the sooner you'll be able to work with number charts easily.

So, that's the story of the Nashville Numbering System, how to use a capo, and the rudiments of how to transpose. It may take you awhile to think, speak, and play by numbers instead of letters, but I guarantee your time will be well spent. Any work you do on the numbering system will increase your understanding of our larger system of music. The more you understand, the better you'll hear and play and the more fun you'll have, with or without the bad jokes! Which reminds me, a kangaroo, a penguin and a horse walk into a grocery store. Clerk says, "Hey, is this some kind of joke?"

You can reach me at: Musix, P.O. Box 231005, Pleasant Hill, CA 94523 (e-mail: musix1@aol.com). Musix has all my CDs, videos, and instructional books and tapes.

Good luck!
Dix Bruce, Fall 2000